DOCTOR F

Christopher Marlowe's

# DOCTOR FAUSTUS

in a new version by
Edwin Morgan

CANONGATE BOOKS

First published in Great Britain in 1999 by
Canongate Books Ltd, 14 High Street,
Edinburgh EH1 1TE

10 9 8 7 6 5 4 3 2 1

The publishers acknowledge subsidy from the Scottish Arts Council
towards the publication of this volume.

*British Library Cataloguing-in-Publication Data*
A catalogue record for this book is available on
request from the British Library

ISBN 0 86241 989 1

Typeset by Hewer Text Ltd, Edinburgh
Printed and bound by The Cromwell Press, Trowbridge, Wiltshire

Edwin Morgan, Stakis Scottish Writer of the Year, was commissioned by TAG Theatre Company in 1999 to write a new version of the classic story of *Doctor Faustus* written in the 16<sup>th</sup> century by Christopher Marlowe.

This play received its World Premiere at Paisley Arts Centre on Thursday 2 September 1999 and toured across Scotland.

Director    James Brining
Designer    Madeleine Millar
Assistant Director    Bruce Strachan
Lighting Designer    Paul Sorley
Composer    David Goodall

Cast

Cora Bissett – Chorus, Scholar, Wagner, Mephistopheles, Vatican Guard, Sultan

Ralph Bolland – Chorus, Scholar, Cornelius, Mephistopheles, Devilish Wife, Beelzebub, Pope, Sultan's wife

Kenneth Harvey – Chorus, Scholar, Valdes, Mephistopheles, Lucifer, Sultan's wife

Dawn Reid – Chorus, Scholar, Mephistopheles, Bruno, Vatican priest, Vizier, Helen of Troy

Ali de Souza – Dr Faustus

**TAG** TAG Theatre Company is Scotland's national theatre company for young people

*Doctor Faustus* was commissioned with funding from the Scottish Arts Council   THE SCOTTISH **ARTS** COUNCIL

*The Cast*

Chorus
Dr Faustus
Wagner, *his apprentice*
Valdes ⎱
Cornelius ⎰ *his friends, experimenters*
Three Scholars, *students under Faustus*
Old Man

The Pope
Giordano Bruno, *the philosopher*
Vatican Guard
Priest

The Sultan of Constantinople
His Vizier
Sultan's two Wives
A Genie

Good Angel
Bad Angel
Mephistopheles
Lucifer
Beelzebub
Spirits *representing*
  The Seven Deadly Sins
  The Seven Deadly Things
  Helen of Troy
Various Devils

Scene: Wittenberg, Rome, Constantinople

# Prologue

CHORUS

Good people, this is not a tale of wars,
Of guns and trumpets, charges, victories,
Nor is it a melting love-romance
With dainty dalliance on rich divans.
No, we are here to tell you the strange story
Of John Faustus, born poor in Germany,
A brilliant boy who made his way to college,
Studied in Wittenberg, amazed his masters
By scaling the heights of theology and science
And graduating as a doctor of renown.
Not the world but the universe was his oyster.
What would he do? What could he not do?
Watch and listen, as his mind is set to soar
Into far regions unexplored before.

## Act One *Scene One*

FAUSTUS IN HIS STUDY

FAUSTUS

Learning is my life – I must take stock of it.
I have studied, graduated, I am Dr Faustus,
But what do gowns and parchments really tell us?
What is my niche, my specialty, my dream?
Philosophy? I once thought that would do the trick:
By argument, to tie an opponent in knots,

1

By logic, to prove black was really white,
By speculation, to pace the boundaries
Of being and non-being. Wonderful!
I tried it, I knew it, I was there!
So what? The earth went round just as before.
Philosophers have only interpreted the world,
The point is to change it.

What about medicine?
A cure for every sickness in the body?
Dr Faustus has it! The fame! The wealth!
Who has not heard of my prescriptions, my precepts?
Have I not sent plagues packing, saved cities,
Wrestled some wretched maladies into the ground?
Yes and yes; but, but. We are still mortal.
I am poor Dr Faustus, and a man.
If I could make men live eternally,
Or if they died, give them a second life,
Then I could worship medicine. Without that,
I say good riddance to pills and jabs and plasters.

What next then – law? There's a noble thing.
Leave the same legacy to two different people,
And listen to the brains rattle. It'll cost you
To know what happens. What happens? Oh,
Give one the gift, the other gets its value.
Can you work that out? Isn't it brilliant?
And can a father disinherit his son?

No no unless except etcetera –
A world of pettifogging petty disputes,
A nest of inky-fingered mercenary drudges,
A quorum of slaves and superficial trash!
Faustus was made for better things.

Divinity!

Surely divinity is good, better, best!
Where is my bible, my testament? Let's see,
I open it at random for a sign.
*The wages of sin is death*. Oh that is hard.
Let me try again, at a different place.
*If we say we have no sin, we deceive ourselves,*
*And there is no truth in us.* So we sin,
And so we die, is that it, is that all?
Ah but our death is an everlasting thing.
Is that what you want, Faustus? Dying
For ever? Black book of intimidation,
Black book of predestination, I close you
With a snap. Farewell theology!

I think only science is truly divine,
Physics and metaphysics both, powers
Of prophecy, magic of imagination,
Angles, equations, codes, experiments,
Books of this restless age and ages to come –
These are what I dream of and desire.
Knowledge is the great prerogative

Of being human; animals and nature
Are only sketches of the consciousness
That man must reach and reap and revel in,
An understanding of all things, a destiny!
O what a world of profit and delight,
Of power, of honour, of omnipotence,
Is promised to the learned experimenter!
All things that move between the quiet poles
Shall be at my command. Emperors and kings
May win obedience where their writ extends,
But hurricane and lightning laugh at them.
The scientist is king in his own land,
Which runs to the utmost grasp of the mind of man.
Good scientists are gods. I'll be a god.
That's the divinity I'll fix my brain on.

ENTER WAGNER

Wagner, commend me to my dearest friends,
Valdes and Cornelius, ask them to visit me.

WAGNER

I will sir, at once.

(EXIT)

FAUSTUS

What they have to say
Will help me hugely in my projected quest.

ENTER GOOD ANGEL AND BAD ANGEL

GOOD. A.

O Faustus, shut that book of devilish science.

Science can tempt the soul. Close those pages,
Do you want God to blast you with his anger?
Read, read your bible, not that blasphemy!

BAD A.

Go forward Faustus in that splendid study
Where nature's treasures lie in wait for you.
You can be a god on earth, not in the sky,
Lord of the atoms and the elements.

EXEUNT ANGELS

FAUSTUS

I am almost drunk thinking of this.
Spirits of the elements at my beck and call?
Answers to all queries and grey areas?
Spirits to send out on desperate ventures?
I'll have them fly to India for gold,
Ransack the ocean for unblemished pearls,
Plunder new-found America for fruits,
New fruits and sweets, all toothsome priceless things.
I'll have them read me strange philosophy,
Tell me state secrets, no matter where.
I'll have them wall all Germany with brass,
And make the Rhine ripple round Wittenberg.
I'll have them fill the colleges with silk,
To see the students smart and happy at last. *Good
I'll have them pay an army I shall muster
To drive every invader from our shores
And leave me as the ruler of these provinces. *Bad

And yes, I'll have them bend and sweat to invent
More terrible war-machines than the fireships
We have seen ramming and burning bridges.
– Come in, Valdes and Cornelius,
Talk to me, strengthen me with your wisdom.

ENTER VALDES AND CORNELIUS

Dear friends, you have won me over at last.
Science cannot be too arcane for me,
I want it. Not your advice alone
But fierce imagination filled my head
With visions of prophetic mastery.
Philosophy is odious and obscure;
Medicine and law cater for pygmy minds;
Divinity is worst of all the four,
Harsh, disagreeable, contemptible, a sink.
It is science, science that has ravished me!
Good friends, you must keep me on this track,
And I that have dashed and disorientated
Priests and pastors with my deadly dialectic
And got the academic elite of Wittenberg
Swarming to my seminars as swarms of spirits
Clustered to Orpheus when he came to hell,
Will work as many wonders as Agrippa
Who startled Europe with his spooks and fetches.

VALDES

Faustus, these books, your brains, and our experience
Will someday make saints of the three of us.

As Inca and Aztec bow to the power of Spain,
So shall the spirits of the elements
Obey and serve us, whatever we may command.
If we want guarding, they shall be lions,
Or German cavalrymen with lances,
Or Lapland giants trotting by our sides.
Sometimes they'll be like women, wives, virgins
Shadowing more beauty in their airy brows
Than you would find in the white breasts of Venus.
From Venice they will drag huge argosies,
And from America the stream of gold
That almost chokes the coffers of old Spain.
All this will happen, if you are resolute.

FAUSTUS

Valdes, don't question me. My mind is fixed
For power as yours is fixed for life itself.

CORN.

The miracles that science can perform
Will make you vow to study nothing else.
The man that's grounded in astronomy,
In languages, in the earth sciences,
Has everything his progress needs or wants.
Faustus, follow the scientific dream
And you will be more famous, more sought after
Than any sphinx or oracle or shaman.
The spirits tell me they can dry the sea
And raise the treasure of all foreign wrecks;

They've access to whatever hoards of riches
Our ancestors once buried deep in the earth.
Can there be anything forbidden to us three?

FAUSTUS

Nothing, Cornelius! Oh this cheers my soul!
Show me now the experimental method.
Take me to some shaded secret place
Where I can try my hands-on hours of joy.

VALDES

Yes, there are groves of learning you must go to,
Laboratories devoted to Roger Bacon,
Albertus Magnus, other pioneers
Of early science. And don't forget the word:
In the beginning was the word. What else?
Bear with us, we hide nothing from you.

CORN.

Valdes, you are right about the word.
Language is the key to all procedures.
Faustus must sound his way, step by step.

VALDES

Right. The basics, and then more, we'll give him.

FAUSTUS

Join me for dinner, my friends, and after meat
We'll tease out every strand of the great project.
Before I go to sleep, I'll make a start
With my research, though I should die for it.

EXEUNT OMNES

## Act One *Scene Two*

ENTER TWO SCHOLARS

1 SCHOLAR

I wonder what's happened to Faustus? The whole college used to resound to his cries of 'There you have it, gentlemen!'

2 SCHOLAR

We shall soon know; here comes his boy.

ENTER WAGNER, CARRYING WINE

1 SCHOLAR

Wagner boy, where's your master?

WAGNER

God in heaven knows.

2 SCHOLAR

You mean you don't know?

WAGNER

Yes I know, but it doesn't follow, does it?

1 SCHOLAR

Oh, very clever. Just tell us where he is.

WAGNER

That 'just' suggests you cannot argue the case properly, which as scholars you should be able to. Admit you were wrong, and don't lose the place.

2 SCHOLAR

So you won't tell us?

WAGNER

Wrong again: I will tell you. If you were not such dunces you would not ask the question. Is my master not a normal moving physical body? Why should you ask about his location? If I was not by nature phlegmatic, slow to wrath, and prone to lechery – to love, I mean! I would never let you within forty feet of the place of execution, though I confidently expect to see you both hanged there at the next session. Oh well, having wiped the floor with your feeble logic, I will speak with straight thin lips like a man of the cloth: Truly, my dear brethren, my master is inside, executing dinner with Valdes and Cornelius, as this wine, if it could speak, would have told your unobservant honours without asking. And so may the Lord bless you and keep you, my dear brethren.

EXIT

1 SCHOLAR

Valdes and Cornelius! Bad hands to fall into! These are two of the most notorious experimenters.

2 SCHOLAR

Even if Faustus was a stranger and not a friend, I would be worried sick. We had better tell the Rector, to see if anything can be done to save him.

1 SCHOLAR

He may have gone too far already.

2 SCHOLAR

Still, we must try, we can only try. Let's go.

EXEUNT

Act One Scene Three
FAUSTUS IN HIS LABORATORY

FAUSTUS

I stand within the shadow of the night

Which creeps along this earth and gets its cloak
To billow blackly out among the stars
Until Orion blinks and belts it in.
Best is darkness for my secret work!
I mouth my formulas like incantations.
I know experiments are devilish dangerous,
But I must risk what devils lie in wait
As I set out my table of the elements
And circle round it, muttering, adjusting,
Invoking not the known but the unknown,
Deities of incandescent matter,
Spirits of most distant constellations,
Dogs for gods and rats for stars if need be!
Unbelievable things shall be believed!
Earth, air, water, fire, that's fine,
But I must call to what's more elemental
In the black crannies of the universe
To gain the power I need. My help must come
Not from the Lord, he's useless and outmoded,
But from a force and source so dark with danger
I cannot wait to welcome it. It's hellish close!

ENTER A DEVIL

No no, that's horrible! I want a noble spirit
To walk with, work with, talk to. Get away!

EXIT DEVIL

Well now, that was something, it obeyed me!
I am beginning to feel proud and proper.

I am beginning to feel proper powerful.
I want to see a superior shape and servant.
I want to have great Mephistopheles
At my beck and call. I want it now.

ENTER MEPHISTOPHELES

MEPH.

Well Faustus, what would you have me do?

FAUSTUS

You are to wait on me as long as I live
And do whatever Faustus may command.
Get the moon to hit the earth, if need be.
If need be, get the sea to flood the world.

MEPH.

I am a servant to great Lucifer,
And cannot follow you without his leave.
His are the orders we take, not yours.

FAUSTUS

Surely Lucifer made you appear here?

MEPH.

No, I came to you of my own accord.

FAUSTUS

But it was my incantation that summoned you?

MEPH.

That was only the secondary cause,
What makes us fly to catch a glorious soul
Is when we hear some juicy blasphemy,
God called a dog, Christ and Bible trashed.

The one we come to must have done as much
As puts him in some danger of damnation.
All you have to do to summon spirits
Is give the Trinity its books, and sing
A psalm of welcome to the Prince of Darkness.

FAUSTUS

I've done it, O I've done that, I believe
The only Trinity to have real power
Is Lucifer, Beelzebub, and yourself.
These are the three I dedicate my life to.
Damnation? Not a bit of it. All's one,
Hell is Elysium, in afterlife
I'll wander with the old philosophers.
But these are only speculative trifles;
Tell me, your lord Lucifer, what is he?

MEPH.

Arch-regent and commander of all spirits.

FAUSTUS

That Lucifer, was he not once an angel?

MEPH.

Yes Faustus, and God loved him above others.

FAUSTUS

So how could he become a prince of devils?

MEPH.

O through aspiring pride and insolence,
For which God threw him from the face of heaven.

FAUSTUS

And what are you that live with Lucifer?

MEPH.

Unhappy spirits that fell with Lucifer,
Conspired against our God with Lucifer,
And are for ever damned with Lucifer.

FAUSTUS

Where are you damned?

MEPH.

In hell.

FAUSTUS

How can you be in hell, if you are here?

MEPH.

Why this is hell, nor am I out of it.
I saw the face of God, tasted the joys
Of an eternal heaven, can you not think
How I am tortured with ten thousand hells
In being deprived of everlasting bliss?
O Faustus, no more of these frivolous questions,
Which make my soul grow faint, and grue with terror.

FAUSTUS

What, is great Mephistopheles a cry-baby
For simply having lost some heavenly pleasures?
Faustus will teach you how to be a man,
To bid good riddance to futile regrets.
Go to lord Lucifer, tell him how I
Have dared to give myself eternal death

By my impatient taunts and blasphemies:
Tell him he can have my wretched soul
If he will give me good two dozen years
Of science, power, and voluptuousness,
With you at my side, serving me always,
Handing me worldly goods as I may need them,
Handing me knowledge as I may demand it,
To kill my enemies, and help my friends,
And never fail to carry out my will.
Go back with this to your great Lucifer,
Meet me in my laboratory at midnight,
Bring me your master's answer to my offer.

MEPH.

I will Faustus.

EXIT

FAUSTUS

If I had studs and teams of souls like stars
I'd give them all for Mephistopheles.
With him as helper I shall rule the world.
I'll throw a bridge across the restless air
To carry squads of soldiers overseas;
I'll close Gibraltar Straits and fuse new Spain
With ancient Africa, a super-continent
I'll be the king of and take tribute from.
No prince or potentate shall live in peace
Unless I snap my fingers and say 'Right!'
Now that this laboratory is mine

I'll let my scientific dream soar up
Till Mephistopheles comes back again.

EXIT

Act Two Scene One

FAUSTUS IN HIS LABORATORY. MIDNIGHT.

FAUSTUS

My brain burns. If I am to be damned
Is that the end, the end?
Why should I think of either God or heaven?
Give up God, man! Embrace Beelzebub!
I must be firm – no looking backwards, Godwards.
O when I waver I hear a voice in my ears:
'Withdraw from science, turn to God again.'
Yes yes, Faustus will turn to God again.
To God? To somebody who hates me?
The God I serve is my own appetite,
The love I feel is for Beelzebub.
A church I'll build him, and I'll glut the altar
With babies' blood, new-born lukewarm blood.

ENTER THE TWO ANGELS

GOOD A.

Dear Faustus, such a vow is damnable.

FAUSTUS

I am not sorry. Where would repentance get me?

16

GOOD A.

Repentance would set you on the road to heaven.

BAD A.

If you believe that, you would believe anything.

Repentance is illusion, madness, nada.

GOOD A.

Dear Faustus, think of heaven and heavenly things.

BAD A.

No Faustus, think of honour, fame, and wealth.

EXEUNT ANGELS

FAUSTUS

Wealth!

Venice, Hamburg, London will be mine!

What can be done in this world without wealth?

My coffers will be full; my banks will groan;

The citizens will ask and I will say

'Yes' or 'No' or 'Maybe'. I shall sit

In a great chair and twitch my purple robes.

Philanthropy is like a fiery glass.

I'll drink it just to see what happens. Hey!

If Mephistopheles stands by me, gods

Are powerless to hurt me, I am safe.

I have no more doubts. Mephistopheles!

Come with your message from great Lucifer!

Is it not midnight? Come Mephistopheles!

ENTER MEPHISTOPHELES

Tell me what lord Lucifer has decided.

MEPH.

> That I shall wait on Faustus while he lives,
> If he will buy my service with his soul.

FAUSTUS

> But I have already made that promise!

MEPH.

> Ah, but you must bequeath it solemnly,
> Write a deed of gift with your own blood.
> Lucifer insists on that security.
> Without it, I am off to hell at once.

FAUSTUS

> No no, stay. Stay, Mephistopheles.
> Tell me, why does Lucifer want my soul?

MEPH.

> To spread his kingdom.

FAUSTUS

> Is that the reason why he tempts us?

MEPH.

> We suffer less when others suffer too.

FAUSTUS

> You are torturers, can you yourselves feel pain?

MEPH.

> As much as human souls do, yes, we can.
> But come now, am I to have your soul?
> I will wait on you. I will be your slave.
> I will give you more than you can imagine.

FAUSTUS

Aye Mephistopheles, my soul is yours and his.

MEPH.

Stab your arm then, no pussyfooting.
Promise that when a certain day arrives
Your soul is Lucifer's to claim and collect.
This will make you great like Lucifer.

FAUSTUS

It is for love of you I do this now.

[STABS HIS ARM]

My arm is cut, the blood is out, this blood
Flags up my promised soul to Lucifer,
Chief lord and ruler of perpetual night.
Let this red sign make my desire come true.

MEPH.

Words are not enough.
You must write it, write a deed of gift.

FAUSTUS

Aye, so I will.

[WRITES]

But Mephistopheles,
My blood congeals, and I can write no more.

MEPH.

I'll fetch some fire to warm up a free flow.

EXIT

FAUSTUS

Why should my blood go sluggish and then stop?

Is it unwilling I should sign this paper?
It should run, it should stream, I am only halfway!
'Faustus gives you his soul': and there I stuck!
What's wrong with that? My soul's my own to give.
I'll write again: 'Faustus gives up his soul.'

ENTER MEPHISTOPHELES WITH A DISH OF EMBERS

MEPH.

Here, heat the blood on this. There you go.

FAUSTUS

That's fine. It's running freely once again.

[WRITES AS BEFORE]

I shall complete the thing immediately.

MEPH.

What would I not do to win his soul?

FAUSTUS

It is finished. The document is ready.
I have bequeathed my soul to Lucifer.
But what's this written on my arm? *Man,*
*You must fly!* Where could I fly to?
To God? He'll throw me instantly to hell.
The words are gone, there's nothing on my arm.
O yes there is, it's back, it's clear: *Man,*
*You must fly!* I will not, cannot fly!

MEPH.

I'll bring him something to distract his mind.

(EXIT)

FAUSTUS

Tell me, what was all that about?

MEPH.

Nothing Faustus, a little interlude
To show you the pleasures of your new power.

FAUSTUS

But can I raise such spirits if I wish?

MEPH.

Of course, and far far greater spirits too.

FAUSTUS

Some day I'll have them bring back Charlemagne,
Caesar and Cleopatra and all their train,
And then to crown the event, I'll feast my eye
On Helen's blinding beauty, Helen of Troy.
So Mephistopheles, receive this scroll,
My deed of gift, of body and of soul:
Conditional upon your solemn vow
To keep the promises we must share now.

MEPH.

Faustus, I swear by Lucifer and hell
To carry out my part, and do it well.

FAUSTUS

So let me read you the conditions:
*First, that Faustus may be a spirit in form and substance.*

21

*Second, that Mephistopheles shall be his servant to command.*
*Third, that Mephistopheles shall fulfil whatever he is asked.*
*Fourth, that Mephistopheles shall be invisible when required.*
*Fifth, that Mephistopheles shall appear in whatever shape may*
*be required.*

*I, John Faustus of Wittenberg, Doctor, by these presents do*
*give both body and soul to Lucifer, Prince of the East, and to*
*his minister Mephistopheles, and finally grant them, after*
*twenty-four years, the power to carry the said John Faustus,*
*body and soul, flesh, blood, and goods, into their own place,*
*wherever that may be.*

*Signed, John Faustus*

MEPH.

Faustus, do you deliver this as your deed?

FAUSTUS

Aye, take it, and hell mend you! Take it.

MEPH.

How can I help you? Ask away.

FAUSTUS

First I want to know just where is hell?

MEPH.

Under the heavens.

FAUSTUS

Aye, right, so's everything! But where exactly?

MEPH.

Deep in the four elements of nature
Where we are tortured, and remain for ever.

Hell has no limits, it is not walled round
In any place; but where we are is hell,
And where hell is, there we must always be.
Indeed, when the whole universe dissolves
And every creature is purged and purified,
Whatever is not heaven will be hell.

FAUSTUS

I think hell's a fable.

MEPH.

Think that if you like, but you will learn.

FAUSTUS

Why so? Am I hell-bent on damnation?

MEPH.

Of course. Let me just hold up the scroll:
It is written, your soul must go to Lucifer.

FAUSTUS

Aye, and my body too, but what of that?
Do you think I am wet behind the ears?
Do you imagine all these old wives' tales
Of pain after death mean anything to me?

MEPH.

But I am an instance to prove the contrary:
I tell you I am damned, and now in hell.

FAUSTUS

Well, I'll be damned if this looks like hell –
What, eating, sleeping, walking, arguing?
– Let's change the subject. I need to have a wife.

MEPH.

Oh, Faustus, no, let's not mention a wife.

FAUSTUS

Sweet Mephistopheles, get me one: now!

MEPH.

Well, you asked for it. Sit there a moment.
I'll fetch you a wife in the devil's name.

EXIT

ENTER WITH A DEVIL DRESSED LIKE A WOMAN, WITH FIREWORKS

MEPH.

A wife, my Faustus. How do you like her?

FAUSTUS

A bitch, a witch! I'll do without a wife.

MEPH.

Marriage is an empty ceremony.
If you love me, put it out of your mind.
It's mistresses you need, I'll pick them for you,
First quality, I'll bring them to your bed
And when your eye lights up, you choose that one
And have her. She can be as chaste as a saint,
As wise as the Queen of Sheba, as beautiful
As Lucifer the dazzler before his fall,
You will have her.

            – Now take and read this book;
Trace out its formulas if you want wealth,
Join up these charges to raise thunderstorms,
Follow its training of the mental powers

24

And robots will materialize before you,

Ready to do whatever you command.

FAUSTUS

Thanks Mephistopheles. But if I also want to raise spirits like yourself, I shall need another book for that.

MEPH.

No no, it's all here – in these pages – look.

FAUSTUS

I must have a book of astronomy too. I want to learn all about the orbits and configurations of the stars and planets, everything that's up there.

MEPH.

Here they are in this book.

[GIVES SECOND BOOK]

FAUSTUS

Only one more: botany, ecology, the whole green world from the spice-beds of Java to the forests of Bavaria.

MEPH.

Here it is.

[GIVES THIRD BOOK]

FAUSTUS

Surely not – in this slim volume?

MEPH.

Of course it's all there. Would I deceive you?

EXEUNT, LOOKING AT BOOKS

## Act Two *Scene Two*

ENTER TWO SCHOLARS

1 SCHOLAR

Have you seen anything of our good Doctor Faustus?

2 SCHOLAR

I stood outside his laboratory and watched for hours.
You know our Rector told us we must keep him under
observation as closely as we could, because he was under such
danger. Not so easy to do! His lab door is kept firmly locked,
and all we see is his shadow moving behind the window.

1 SCHOLAR

He is alone?

2 SCHOLAR

Sometimes we see Wagner, his apprentice, adjusting an
instrument. And sometimes – it's hard to believe—

1 SCHOLAR

What—?

2 SCHOLAR

There is a third figure, dark, man or woman I don't know.
It does not enter, does not leave, but it is not always there.

1 SCHOLAR

It must be Valdes, or Cornelius?

2 SCHOLAR

No no, I would recognize them. It is like an alien visitor, not
quite human.

1 SCHOLAR

You think—?

**2 SCHOLAR**

I think there are dark forces in nature, and Faustus is in touch with them. Sometimes there are wild bangs and flashes.

**1 SCHOLAR**

That could be an experiment.

**2 SCHOLAR**

Could be, could be. But my flesh crawled when I saw that third person standing at the window and then, the next moment, not to be seen.

**1 SCHOLAR**

Perhaps our Faustus has discovered some new force, a new power in science to promote invisibility?

**2 SCHOLAR**

It is not impossible. But if so, who was it he made invisible? We are no further forward until we know that.

**1 SCHOLAR**

We must tell the Rector, and ask him what we can do. Our Doctor is a good man, but good men sometimes have their eyes on the stars and stumble into traps.

**2 SCHOLAR**

Come then, let us go.

**EXEUNT**

Act Two *Scene Three*

**ENTER FAUSTUS IN HIS LABORATORY, AND MEPHISTOPHELES**

**FAUSTUS**

The sky and the stars, the heavens and their lights –

If I am never to see them, I am lost.

This is your damnable doing, Mephistopheles!

MEPH.

You know fine well you have yourself to blame.

Anyhow, what is so wonderful about the heavens?

Those points of light are far less beautiful

Than you, or any man that breathes on earth.

FAUSTUS

How can that be?

MEPH.

The heavens were made for man; he is superior.

FAUSTUS

If they were made for man, that includes me.

I will renegue from science, and repent.

ENTER THE TWO ANGELS

GOOD A.

Faustus repent; God can still pity you.

BAD A.

You are demonized; God cannot pity you.

FAUSTUS

Who buzzes in my ears that I'm a demon?

If I am a demon, God could pity me.

God could pity me if I repent.

BAD A.

Aye, but Faustus never shall repent.

EXEUNT ANGELS

FAUSTUS

My heart's so hardened I cannot repent!
The very words salvation, faith, and heaven
Are drowned in voices if I utter them,
And 'Damned, Faustus, damned' echoes and re-echoes.
Swords, knives, guns, poison, noose and venom'd steel
Are laid beside me to dispatch myself.
And why should I not, except that pleasures
Deeper than despair swim through my memory.
What powers are already given me!
I have seen and heard old heroes pass before me
As on a screen, but more dimensional.
Did I not get great blind Homer with his harp
To sing of Odysseus and Helen of Troy?
Did I not watch the city walls of Thebes
Fly stone by stone together as its king
Made magic music with Mephistopheles?
Why should I die then, or feebly despair?
No, I will not repent, that's flat, that's clear.
– Come Mephistopheles, let our minds engage.
I have high questions on high astronomy.
Tell me, how many spheres surround the moon?
Do all celestial bodies make one globe
As the four elements make a globe of the earth?

MEPH.

All's one, elements below, sky above.
Our moon, and up to the highest of the heavens,

A nest of shimmering concentric spheres,
All sweetly move upon one axle-tree
Which is a single pole for earth and heaven.
The stars are fixed, but Mars, Jupiter and Saturn
Wander upon a planetary path.

FAUSTUS

Is that one path, one motion and one speed?

MEPH.

An earthly day is not a day in the zodiac.

FAUSTUS

My boy Wagner could have answered that!
Surely Mephistopheles can do better.
Everyone knows planets have double motion:
East to west in a day, but a vaster circle,
Moon in a month, Venus and Mercury a year,
Sun in a year, Mars in four, Jupiter twelve,
Saturn thirty years. That's freshman stuff;
But tell me, is there a spirit, an intelligence, riding and
guiding every sphere?

MEPH.

Aye.

FAUSTUS

How many spheres are there?

MEPH.

Nine: seven planets, the firmament, and the highest
heaven.

FAUSTUS

No sphere of fire? No sphere of crystal?

MEPH.

Nah, these are fables.

FAUSTUS

Why are there more eclipses in some years than others?

MEPH.

Heavenly bodies move at different speeds. I've told you that already.

FAUSTUS

All right all right. The universe is like—

MEPH.

The universe is not like anything. The universe just is.

FAUSTUS

Is it not big? Is it not beautiful? Is it not well made?

MEPH.

You are a fool. It is not an object.

FAUSTUS

It is not nothing. Once there was nothing, and then it appeared. Who made the universe?

MEPH.

I will not answer that.

FAUSTUS

Sweet Mephistopheles, tell me.

MEPH.

Faustus, don't push me too far.

FAUSTUS

You villain, you swore to tell me anything I asked.

MEPH.

Aye, anything that is not against our kingdom! This is. You are one of the damned, and you should be thinking about hell.

FAUSTUS

I am thinking about God: he made the universe, did he not?

MEPH.

Remember what I said.

EXIT

FAUSTUS

Aye, back to hell, get back, bad spirit!

My misery is my damnation: you caused it.

Is it not too late—?

ENTER THE TWO ANGELS

BAD A.

Too late.

GOOD A.

Never too late, if Faustus will repent.

BAD A.

Repent, and devils will tear you to pieces.

GOOD A.

Repent, and they will never graze your skin.

EXEUNT ANGELS

FAUSTUS

O Christ my saviour, my saviour,

Help me in this distress, help my soul.

ENTER LUCIFER, BEELZEBUB, AND MEPHISTOPHELES

LUCIFER

Christ cannot save your soul, for he is just.

That soul belongs elsewhere now and it is mine.

FAUSTUS

O what a fearsome face! Who are you?

LUCIFER

I am Lucifer, and this is my princely companion in hell.

FAUSTUS

You have both come to fetch my soul!

BEELZEBUB

We have come to warn you that you are injuring us.

LUCIFER

You are calling on Christ, contrary to your promise.

BEELZEBUB

Stop thinking about God.

LUCIFER

Think about the devil.

BEELZEBUB

And his dam. [*gives horrible laugh*]

FAUSTUS

Forgive me, I shall watch my tongue, I swear it.

Never will I raise my sights to heaven,

Never will I pray to God, or name him.

I'll burn his scriptures, kill his ministers,

Make my spirits pull his churches down.

**LUCIFER**

Do it. Show your obedience. We reward
Good servants well and long; you will see it.

**BEELZEBUB**

Faustus, we have come here in person from hell in order to
provide you with some entertainment. Sit down, and you will
see the Seven Deadly Sins passing before you as large as life.

**FAUSTUS**

O I shall enjoy that – just like Adam admiring Paradise on
the first day of his creation.

**LUCIFER**

Shut your mouth about Paradise and creation. You will never
learn, will you? Mephistopheles, bring them in.

ENTER THE SEVEN DEADLY SINS

**BEELZEBUB**

Now Faustus, ask them their names and what they do. You
might learn something in the process. We want to entertain
you: it's sin but it's fun. Put it the other way: it's fun but it's
sin. Were you ever greedy? envious? lecherous? etcetera
etcetera, you know the rest. See if you recognize your
brothers and sisters. See if they recognize you.
Talk to them.

**FAUSTUS**

Certainly. You, the first one, who are you?

**PRIDE**

I am Pride. I disdain to have any parents. I am like the flea
that lords it over a girl's body, creeping into every nook and

cranny: sometimes standing on her brow like a periwig; next, hanging on her neck like a necklace; then, like a feathery fan, I kiss her lips; and finally, I am an embroidered smock and do some close work with her. But goodness, what a stink there is here! I'll not speak another word till someone sprays perfume on the floor and spreads out some really really rich rugs.

FAUSTUS

Well, pride goes before a fall. And the second, who are you?

AVARICE

I am Avarice, and I saw the light of day in an old miser's money-bag. If I had my way, I would magic this whole house and everyone in it to gold. I would spirit you all into my treasure-chest and keep you safe for ever. Gold, all gold, all my darling gold.

FAUSTUS

Very good; I like gold myself. And who is the third?

ENVY

I am Envy. My parents were a chimney-sweep and a fishwife. Because I can't read, I want all books to be burnt. Because I'm poor, I have to watch others eat, and I'd love to see a worldwide famine so that everyone would die except me: then I'd grow fat. And why should I stand when that one's sitting? Tell that one to get off his chair.

FAUSTUS

Not likely! You can envy away. But who's the fourth?

ANGER

I am Anger. I had neither father nor mother: I jumped out of a lion's mouth when I was hardly an hour old, and ever since then I have run up and down the world with this pair of rapiers, wounding myself when I could get no one to fight with. I was born in hell, and respect it, for someone in your hellish company may prove to be my father.

FAUSTUS

I shall keep out of your path. The fifth, there, what are you?

GLUTTONY

I am Gluttony. My parents are dead, and devil a penny they left me except my living expenses, and that's a pittance. All it buys me is thirty meals a day, plus ten snacks: just enough to keep body and soul together. I have a royal pedigree: my father was a huge roll of gammon, and my mother was a hogshead of claret. My godfathers were Peter Pickled-Herring and Martin Marinade-Beef: O but my godmother was a jolly jinky gentlewoman, chucked under the chin wherever she went; she was Mistress Margery Marvel-Beer. Now Faustus, you have heard all about my family; how about inviting me to supper?

FAUSTUS

Supper be hanged! You would eat me out of house and home.

GLUTTONY

Then the devil choke you!

FAUSTUS

Choke yourself, glutton. Who is the sixth?

SLOTH

Ho hum! I am Sloth. I was born on a sunny bank, where I have lain ever since, and you have done very wrong to drag me here. I want to be taken back, pronto. Ho ho hum. I'll not speak another word, not for all the opium in China.

FAUSTUS

Good riddance. You are no use to me. And the seventh and last, who might you be?

LECHERY

Who am I? Who, eh? Can't you guess? I am a minx, a madam, a masseuse. I am one that loves six inches of raw quivering steak better than a long flabby drooping codfish. My name is Le-, Le-, let me see, Lily, no, Lizzie, no, Lezzie, no no, Lesmahagow, no no no, it's Lechery, that's it, that's me, now you know me.

FAUSTUS

I know you, Lechery. Hello and goodbye right now.

LUCIFER

To hell, to hell! Away to hell, all seven!

EXEUNT THE SEVEN DEADLY SINS

FAUSTUS

Amazing, what a vision, can I see more?

LUCIFER

Hell is bursting with delicious shows.

FAUSTUS

To see hell and come back, that would be wonderful.

LUCIFER

Faustus, come midnight I will fulfil your desire. Meanwhile take this book, read it carefully, it will give you power to change your shape at will.

FAUSTUS

Thanks, Lucifer, thanks, great spirit. I shall guard these pages with my life.

LUCIFER

Farewell Faustus, think on the devil.

FAUSTUS

Lucifer, I will. Come Mephistopheles.

EXEUNT ALL, SEVERAL WAYS

Act Two *Scene Four*

ENTER WAGNER WITH A BOOK, VALDES AND CORNELIUS

VALDES

My good Wagner, is your master within?

WAGNER

I am not your good Wagner, I am Dr Faustus's good Wagner. Indeed, my master is within, and you two are without, and you are without any chance of getting within. My master does not want to see Valdes and Cornelius or any other at the moment. Who are you?

CORN.

You know fine well we are Cornelius and Valdes. Now will you let us into the laboratory to see Dr Faustus?

WAGNER

You may be Cornelius and Valdes, but that is no different, as far as my knowledge of logic goes, from Valdes and Cornelius. Therefore, I cannot let you in.

VALDES

This is ridiculous. We are your master's friends and tutors.

WAGNER

You *were* my master's friends and tutors. But Dr Faustus has now gone far beyond anything you can teach him. He is in touch with the basic forces of the cosmos. His own power grows daily, and will soon be seen in the world.

CORN.

I want to hear it from his own lips.

VALDES

We demand to see him. How do we know you have not murdered him and stolen his ideas?

WAGNER

Gentlemen, Faustus breathes as well as you and I do. I have no need to steal his ideas. I am his trusted apprentice and helper. The love he bears me is the power he shares with me.

VALDES

A lab boy! What power does a lab boy have, beyond filling flasks and mixing powders?

WAGNER

You would not believe me if I told you, so I will not tell you.

CORN.

Come Valdes, let's push past him. Faustus must see us. We must speak to him.

WAGNER .

[*Lifts and opens book*] No further, gentlemen. By this book, which I know so well I can read it backwards as well as forwards, I have the power to hex you where you stand. You want to speak to Faustus? What if you could not speak? [*gazes at book for a moment, then points at Valdes and Cornelius*] What if you lost the power of speech? Valdes?

**VALDES**

Mnmmbrm hmbm ng ng bnuh bnuh prmnm prm.

**WAGNER**

What was that? I didn't quite catch that. Maybe Cornelius could translate it for me?

**CORN.**

Kthss wzz wrr skzaw krrwah hhzz zzwaw.

**WAGNER**

I am still in the dark.

**VALDES**

Blnwah! Ng!

**WAGNER**

Losing your temper will not help.

**CORN.**

Sknwa khr khr brzuh brzuh brzuh!

**WAGNER**

I detect a note of desperation. Gentlemen, where is that gift of the gab you had when you thought you could twist my master round your little finger? Language is a glory of the mind, but the glory has departed. What will you do now?

**VALDES**

Blmwah vzah akhgr mnnmm.

**WAGNER**

That will do you no good, will it? You could not even ask a citizen the time of day, far less summon spirits to conjure the good doctor into your presence. Perhaps I shall reverse the spell, perhaps I shall not. Never despise apprentices: they may have access. In the meantime, gentlemen, go to hell. I have work to do.

VALDES ⎫ BRM GHZ WHAWAW . . .
CORN. ⎭ THRR SKHRAW MNUH . . .

**WAGNER**

I said go to hell. Have you no English?

EXEUNT ALL, VARIOUSLY

# Chorus II

CHORUS

This learned Doctor Faustus could not rest
With books, he had to see the world, the stars,
The planets, had to see the universe
And circle with it; his aspiring mind
Became impatient with all boundaries.
From Everest's white peak he saw the sun
Shining like molten gold upon a chariot
Ready to mount into the blue; dragons
Were straining at the bit; he drove off
Slicing by clouds, moon, Mars, Jupiter,
Sphere after sphere, skewing the heavenly pole,
Gliding across the zodiac with his dragons
That one week later snorted him back home.
No rest, no rest! On dragon-back this time
He swept and swivelled low across the earth,
Taking such pictures with his memory
As would engrave both known and secret kingdoms
Deep and safe and filed for future action.
This man of learning learns the art of power!

## Act Three *Scene One*

ENTER FAUSTUS AND MEPHISTOPHELES

FAUSTUS

Ah, what travels, Mephistopheles!
Were we in space, or time? Fortresses,

42

Rivers, vineyards, my head is spinning,
Paris, Naples, ancient fields, new streets,
Mosaics of Venice, Virgil's tomb, they flash
Like spokes of a wheel, a thousand years
And more of Europe. So what now, my friend?
I wanted Rome. Is that where we are now?

MEPH.

It is, my Faustus. We are in the Vatican,
Waiting in a private chamber of the Pope.

FAUSTUS

I trust his holiness will bid us welcome.

MEPH.

Who cares? We are here to do what we want.
As for Rome, do you know what it is like?
A city built on seven hills, the Tiber
Cutting it in two, bridged over four times,
With castles, cannons, obelisks, huge gates –
Oh, there is plenty to wonder at, my friend.

FAUSTUS

By God, I mean by hell, by the burning lake
And by the river of the damned, I swear
I have to see this city's monuments.
Let us go out among them.

MEPH.

                              Not yet, my Faustus.
You wanted to see the Pope, you'll see the Pope.
Any time now, he will be here. Let us wait.

FAUSTUS

Oh yes, oh yes, I want to see the Pope.
Sweet Mephistopheles, you read my mind.
I want, I want, what do I not want?
While I am here on earth, let me be cloyed
With all things that delight the heart of man.
Two dozen years of liberty are mine
To spend in pleasure and to glut my senses
Until my name is beaten like a gong
Throughout the European universe.

MEPH.

Well said, my Faustus; live, and see, and do.

FAUSTUS

I think to do is better than to see.
Good Mephistopheles, remember how
We viewed the face of heaven, of earth and hell,
Within the eight days of our voyaging:
Our dragons soared so high into the air
That I looked down upon a shrunken earth
No bigger than my hand; our sight took in
The patchwork of the kingdoms of the globe.
The pleasure of the eye was filled and sated.
But now I want some action, and the Pope
Must feel it. Find ways of doing this!

MEPH.

I can, I will. We shall hoodwink the Pope
By rescuing his major enemy,

His prisoner, the great Giordano Bruno
And now pronounced a dangerous heretic.

FAUSTUS

Bruno the scientist, the philosopher,
Not Bruno that fearless illuminator?

MEPH.

He may himself illuminate a city
If he is brought to the stake. We must help him.
He is one of us.

FAUSTUS

His head is like a star.
I know his works. Tell me what we must do.

MEPH.

I have a plan. The Pope comes here with Bruno,
Probes him with questions for a recantation,
Threatens horrors. Bruno will not recant.
In the meantime we disappear, put on
The vestments of two cardinals—

FAUSTUS

Oh yes!—

MEPH.

And on a summons from the Pope—

FAUSTUS

A bell!—

MEPH.

We join the ineffably infallible one,
Denounce the mad star-gazing heretic

And take him away to painful execution –
Except that once we've left the Vatican
We'll strike off Bruno's fetters, muffle him up,
Send him by secret roads to Germany
Where he'll be free to publish his researches
Unhampered by the mitre and the faggot.
What say you, my Faustus, shall we be cardinals?

FAUSTUS

Every inch, good Mephistopheles. Lead on.

EXEUNT FAUSTUS AND MEPHISTOPHELES

ENTER THE POPE, AND GIORDANO BRUNO IN CHAINS

POPE

The Inquisition has not left you bowed.

BRUNO

I have been interrogated. I live.

POPE

It is only by extreme graciousness
That I have summoned you into this chamber,
Where we may sift some questions face to face.

BRUNO

The only favour you could show to me
Would be to file my chains and set me free.

POPE

I am not angered by your truculence,
I see it as a sickness in your soul
Which might have been plucked out but flourishes
In self-assured conceit and arrogance.

Bruno, you suffer from the primal sin.

Pride it was that brought down Lucifer.

BRUNO

I have the pride of an enquiring spirit.

No one can ever tell me that is bad.

POPE

Your job is not to enquire, but to obey.

Do you imagine the Doctors of the Church –

And I say nothing of the Holy Fathers –

Have failed to set out every point of faith

Needed for salvation? Who are you

To say there are multiple worlds, many Christs,

Evolutions of unfinished space and time?

Augustine and Aquinas, were they fools?

BRUNO

No, but they could not guess what we know now.

Copernicus has smashed the mouldering lectern.

World upon world now rises into view.

Some other earth may be the chosen place,

And Jesus Christ may have to bleed there too.

POPE

Be careful, Bruno. These are dangerous thoughts.

BRUNO

We live in a whole universe of danger.

Nothing is set in a mould for ever.

POPE

God made the world, and saw that it was good.

BRUNO

Did he? I think the universe evolved
And is evolving, and is infinite.
Not even God could render it finite.

POPE

Our very senses show us the fixed limits,
Even if God had not decreed them first.
Sun rises, sets; don't we have calendars?

BRUNO

Our senses tell us many untrue things.
Do sun and moon rise and set to please us?
Are we the centre of the universe?
What would you see if we were standing on the sun?
Would you not watch an earth rise from the moon?
All things are relative, even truth.
A Pope on Mars might curse this piddling earth
If he could catch it whizzing round the sun!

POPE

No one is on Mars. Mars is a light in the sky.

BRUNO

Millions of worlds are either inhabited
Or waiting to be so. This we shall find out.

POPE

To seek forbidden knowledge is great sin.
That way damnation lies.

BRUNO

I think not.

O nothing is forbidden to human greatness!

There are no limits to the mind of man!

POPE

So be it then. You are a proud bad spirit.

You are condemned out of your own mouth.

You are bound for a pit, unless extraordinary mercy,

Which we must always pray for, should descend.

Cardinals! *Rings bell*

ENTER FAUSTUS AND MEPHISTOPHELES AS CARDINALS

FAUSTUS

Your holiness, we are at your command.

You have interrogated the prisoner?

POPE

Take him away. His soul, beyond redemption,

Utters such blasphemies my ears are soiled.

FAUSTUS

You gave him one last chance out of your grace.

The holy synod of bishops and archbishops

Has been unanimous in its decree:

That this Giordano Bruno has been marked

As a bold heretic and black example to all,

A proud disturber of the Church's peace,

A hive of diabolic speculations,

And one, in short, in whom they find no good.

If he persists in his unnatural course,

Unmoved by reason, torture, or authority,
He shall be tagged with insolent heresy,
And on a pile of faggots burnt to death.

POPE

It is enough: here, take him to your charge,
And set him in the deepest lockfast dungeon
Until tomorrow's most collegiate session
Of gravest cardinals gives his grave crimes
A solemn outcome into life or death.
With this, the papal blessing is upon you.

EXIT POPE

MEPH.

A devil blessed by the Pope, whatever next!

FAUSTUS

Come, Bruno, we are not cardinals
But seekers after knowledge like yourself.
We shall disguise you, we have horses waiting
To speed you on your way to Germany.
Be vigilant. Trust no one. Keep the course.
Blindness and bigotry fly after you.
Try London if Wittenberg is perilous;
We have friends there. Let us go.

MEPH.

Come, come.

EXEUNT FAUSTUS, MEPHISTOPHELES, AND BRUNO

## Act Three *Scene Two*

ENTER FAUSTUS AND MEPHISTOPHELES IN THEIR OWN SHAPES.

INDISTINCT BUT ANGRY SHOUTING IS HEARD IN THE DISTANCE.

FAUSTUS

I think the Pope knows that the bird has flown.

MEPH.

But where are the cardinals who set it free?

FAUSTUS

*That* he'll never know! [*they laugh*] Let's have some fun.

His inexpressible altitude is coming,

I hear his steps. Dear Mephistopheles,

Let us put on cloaks of invisibility

And give the Pope a taste of things uncouth.

MEPH.

It shall be done. With these, we are unseen

By mortal men. Be quick, for there he is.

[THEY PUT ON CLOAKS]

ENTER POPE AND A VATICAN GUARD

POPE

By heaven I'll have someone's head for this.

Bruno, that vile heretic, escaped –

Gone to spread his poison over Europe –

How could it happen? You, the Vatican guard,

The elite, the professionals, let the devil slip

From your butter fingers, I'll fire you all.

FAUSTUS

[*loud whisper in* POPE's *ear*] I'm a fireball!

POPE

Who said that? Who spoke?

GUARD

Not me, your holiness,
And if I may dare to say to your holiness
We only let the miscreant Bruno through
Because two cardinals commanded it.

POPE

These cardinals we cannot find. Where are they?

FAUSTUS

[*in* POPE's *ear*] They are here.

POPE

What in God's name— Guard, are you up to some
Circus ventriloquism, is it carnival time?
There are only two of us here.

FAUSTUS

[*in* POPE's *ear*] Hear, hear!

GUARD

[*crossing himself*] Your holiness, it has to be a spirit.
There are always evil spirits where goodness is.

POPE

Hm, well. Evil is always active.
I have never myself yet seen a demon,
But you do not have to see a demon to hear one.
As it is written, the devil is at large on this earth.
When cardinals vanish and heretics run free,
It may be human guards are powerless

Before some supernatural assault. If so,
No blame attaches to you. You may go.
Tell my special chapel priest to prepare
Bell, book, and candle for an exorcism.

FAUSTUS

[*in* POPE's *ear*] Better try an orgasm.

POPE

Saints and angels, it gets worse! Hurry, hurry!

EXIT GUARD

Dear God, if I have flouted any commandment,
Even the least of those you have given us,
I here and now repent and beg for grace.
Let not the hungry hordes of hell be loosed
To feed on my confusion with their babblement.
I did my best to send Bruno to the flames
And keep your doctrine free from his pollution.
Do not hold it against me, Lord, that he
By some unearthly means escaped. Help me
To keep Rome clean and pure and everlasting.

ENTER PRIEST AS EXORCIST, WITH BELLS,
BOOK, AND CANDLE

PRIEST

I curse whoever organized the freeing of Giordano Bruno
from just custody. I curse him or them and I shall not leave
cursing.

FAUSTUS

[*still invisible*] Bless them all.

PRIEST

I curse whoever uttered vile words in the ear of our holy
father the Pope and distracted him from his divine work. I
curse him or them and I shall not leave cursing.

FAUSTUS

[*invisible*] Bless them all.

PRIEST

I curse that wicked spirit which seeks to interrupt and
arrogantly to contradict the very maledictions I am uttering
in the name of the Lord. I curse him or them and I shall not
leave cursing.

FAUSTUS

[*invisible*] Bless him, bless them, bless them all.

FAUSTUS AND MEPHISTOPHELES SHOUT AND THROW
FIREWORKS. IN THE DIN AND SMOKE, POPE AND PRIEST FLEE
IN TERROR, PURSUED BY FAUSTUS AND MEPHISTOPHELES.
EXEUNT.

# Chorus III

CHORUS

Our Faustus now is famed in many lands.

The tongues of Europe wag at his exploits.

Astronomers and theologians

Throw questions at him about stars and fate,

Mars and faith, heaven and the heavens,

And patiently he teases out the rigours

Of religion, asks his questions in return.

His knowledge burns some fingers, warms some hearts.

Kings, emperors, and popes will all ignore him

At their peril. He travels like the wind

And no one sees him go. As many rumours

As would settle like birds in a huge hall

Follow and surround him. Has he a partner?

Yes. No. Sometimes. Perhaps. Who knows?

From mystery, power grows. He is that man

Who once aspired to learn all hidden things

And now would crown himself with Saturn's rings.


## Act Four *Scene One*

ENTER TWO SCHOLARS

1 SCHOLAR

I have a letter from Dr Faustus.

2 SCHOLAR

What a long time since we heard from him! Where has he
been? Is he safe and well?

1 SCHOLAR

He has been travelling – France, Italy, up mountains, God knows where. He says he has been in courts and palaces, been welcomed by great men, given special favours, been praised as the most learned man in Europe. He says, 'If I was to tell you all my adventures, you would not believe me.'

2 SCHOLAR

And what about his science, his research?

1 SCHOLAR

I get the impression that all that is behind him: he seems to have reached such a stage of dominion over nature that he can apply his research to wonderful works in the world.

2 SCHOLAR

Water into wine, you mean, that kind of thing?

1 SCHOLAR

Oh, that would be nothing, all in the day's work, if what he writes is true. He says it is not impossible to become invisible, and he has done so, though with help from some other, whom he does not identify.

2 SCHOLAR

This is worrying. I am thinking of that shadowy figure in his laboratory.

1 SCHOLAR

Indeed. There is a whiff of sulphur somewhere.

2 SCHOLAR

He was so eager to do good, to us, to the university, to

Wittenberg, to Germany. Surely he cannot have allowed himself to be sidetracked into devious courses.

1 SCHOLAR

I am sure the old Faustus we knew and loved is still there. But this letter seems to come from a new Faustus. There is a boastful tone about his stories of conquest and wonder-working. It is as if he had never heard that the first of the Seven Deadly Sins is Pride. And yet, with all that crowing and careering and congratulating of himself, I detect a strange unease, almost a fear, as if he had gone out into some weird uncharted territory and might never find his way back.

2 SCHOLAR

He has money?

1 SCHOLAR

Oh, money. Gold, silver, dollars, jewels, you name it. He has been showered with gifts, from Scotland to Russia.

2 SCHOLAR

So perhaps we worry too much.

1 SCHOLAR

No, we do not worry too much. I sense something which I cannot describe, but which is not good. I think we should pray for him.

2 SCHOLAR

And when shall we see Faustus again?

1 SCHOLAR

It may be quite a while. The letter says, 'We leave (notice the "we") – we leave tomorrow for Constantinople.' Come, let us tell the other scholars.

EXEUNT


## Act Four *Scene Two*
### CONSTANTINOPLE. THE SULTAN'S PALACE.
#### ENTER THE SULTAN AND HIS VIZIER

SULTAN

I understand we have a visitor.

VIZIER

Indeed we have, my lord, he comes from Europe.
Faustus is his name; he is a doctor.

SULTAN

Doctor of what? Medicine? Philosophy?

VIZIER

That is not clear. There are many rumours and stories.
It is said he is a great scholar, and rich.

SULTAN

A scholar, and rich? There's a phenomenon!
I presume he has letters of introduction.

VIZIER

From kings and generals and scientists.

SULTAN

Generals, eh? He is a man of power?

VIZIER

Some say he has unlimited powers.

SULTAN

Who can believe that? However, we shall test him.

Has he servants, an entourage, a wife?

VIZIER

He has a companion, Mephistopheles.

The two are thought to be inseparable.

SULTAN

Interesting, interesting. Bring them in.

VIZIER

I will, my lord.

EXIT VIZIER

ENTER FAUSTUS AND MEPHISTOPHELES, WITH VIZIER

SULTAN

Welcome to Turkey,

To Constantinople, and this my palace

Where you shall find how well we treat our guests.

FAUSTUS

Our gratefulness will be made evident.

We have brought gifts, the cream of the west,

Books, elixirs, scientific instruments,

Everything to please aspiring minds,

Amaze your subjects, and extend your power.

SULTAN

Faustus, that pleases us. We shall talk further.

– And this, sir, must be Mephistopheles.

MEPH.

At your service. You have a fine place here.

SULTAN

Order and beauty and dominion –
Where I live, I like to have all three.
I am sustained in this by my vizier.

VIZIER

[bows] Gentlemen.

FAUSTUS

I was consumed by curiosity
To see your city. Its fame is great
And yet it is unknown, secret, strange.

SULTAN

We think it is the centre of the world.
Ancient majestic Asia, turbulent Europe
Mingle and chatter here with a dozen tongues.
Constantinople is water and gold.
Our domes and minarets gleam in the sun,
Our ferries thread a maze of seas, our galleys
Harry Venice, our pirates have gold earrings.

FAUSTUS

And yet you might make more gold if you wished.

SULTAN

How can that be? Gold is mined, not made.

FAUSTUS

All matter has constituent elements
Invisible to the eye; once discovered,
These atoms are ready for manipulation.
Everything in nature can be made by man.

VIZIER

[*to* SULTAN] My lord, this is not possible. Science
Has dreamed for ages of turning lead to gold.
It is a joke. Or else it is devilish.

SULTAN

Devilish clever, my vizier. An open mind
Is best when we consider basic things.
The universe is surely all one stuff –
Stars and sandgrains, lakes, crows, trees –
There is no break, no discontinuity –
Allah (praised be his name) breathes through it all.

MEPH.

We do not need Allah.

FAUSTUS

Or God.

VIZIER

Or Satan?

Unlawful things are best kept dungeon-deep.

FAUSTUS

But who lays down the law? All things are possible.
Everything possible to be done will be done.
The boundless human brain will take no less.

SULTAN

Dr Faustus, you are a man of vision.
We shall continue our conversation.
But it grows late. I must bid you goodnight.
My vizier will show you your quarters in a moment.

SULTAN

What do you think?

VIZIER

                                 Well, I think the Doctor
Soars too near the sun and will scorch his wings.

SULTAN

And the other?

VIZIER

                        Says little, but I do not trust him.

SULTAN

You think they are spies?

VIZIER

                              Anyone from the west
May be a spy. We have useful secrets,
Military, technical. Who knows what they want?

SULTAN

Letters of recommendation from crowned heads?

VIZIER

They could be forged. These two could forge anything.

SULTAN

You are very sure about this. Why so?

VIZIER

They are neither Muslim nor Christian nor Jew,
So what are they? I feel something shadowy,
Something dark, not quite human, about them.
Did you see the way they looked at each other?

As if in league? My duty is to protect you,
My lord. That is why I am vigilant.
There are enemies of flesh and blood,
And there are enemies who are demons,
As the Holy Koran tells us.

SULTAN

                              I know it
And I am grateful. Watch them carefully.
At our next audience, make sure the bottle is there.
We shall see if the genie has anything to tell us.
And now goodnight.

VIZIER

                      I hear and I obey.

EXEUNT


Act Four *Scene Three*

THE HAREM. ENTER TWO OF THE SULTAN'S WIVES

1 WIFE

Who is it tonight?

2 WIFE

O it is Fatima.

1 WIFE

She is well named. Have you seen her waistline recently?

2 WIFE

Yes, but he once told me that is what he likes. 'You can keep your
skinny ones,' he said, 'your models, your anorexics. I love to dive
into a pneumatic sea, to flounder and bounce and drown there in

the midst of those pearly folds.' That's what he said, believe it or not. I tried to put on some weight after that, I can tell you.

1 WIFE

He's a big man – I mean – big.

2 WIFE

Well, he gives satisfaction. He fulfils. He takes his time and he knows what a woman wants.

1 WIFE

You'll give him a reference? [*they laugh*]

2 WIFE

I doubt if he wants to leave us. Look at how well he keeps us supplied: perfumes and oils, jasmine, sandalwood, vetiver, fine soaps, fluffy towels, endless baths, fish and lamb, wine and grapes, and oh those lovely melting chunks of pink and lemon rahat lokum!

1 WIFE

Steady on! I'm starving. It's about time the eunuch brought our supper.

2 WIFE

Did you manage to see the two visitors?

1 WIFE

Nothing's hidden here. I caught a glimpse of them through the grille.

2 WIFE

What did you think?

1 WIFE

Well, I could go the doctor, but I didn't fancy his friend.

2 WIFE

I was the opposite. I thought the doctor was a bit – intellectual. But his friend was kinda magnetic in an interesting, sinister sort of way – he could probably make you do things you'd never done before.

1 WIFE

Lick his boots? Hand him the whip?

2 WIFE

No, I don't think so. I don't know. It's just something about him, something hard to resist—

1 WIFE

Anyway, you can't have him. So think of supper instead.

2 WIFE

Let's go and see what that snail of a eunuch is doing.

EXEUNT


Act Four *Scene Four*

THE PALACE. MORNING. CRY OF MUEZZIN.

ENTER FAUSTUS AND MEPHISTOPHELES

MEPH.

Did you sleep, my Faustus, in this strange land?

FAUSTUS

I slept until I heard the muezzin call.

MEPH.

Better than church bells.

FAUSTUS

Worse than church bells!

I can see these bottoms lifted in the air,
Lips muttering and grovelling in the dust.
What slaves those Muslims are! Never so bold
As to be damned! Submission, submission!
We could shake them awake, could we not?

MEPH.

You would think the Sultan was worse than the Pope.

FAUSTUS

Not really. But I hate that sense of fate.
'It is written.' How do they know it is written?

MEPH.

May I remind you of what you once wrote
In your own blood. That is not forgotten
And will be fulfilled until the end of time
And beyond the end of time. Think of that.

FAUSTUS

O Mephistopheles, you drive nails into me!
I will repent, I will repent, I will!
Nothing is ever too late for God!

MEPH.

Do not mention God, or Allah. Think of Lucifer
Who is more glorious in being unglorified.
– In the meantime think of the Sultan:
He will soon be here. Calm down.
Be sharp. We devils may learn something.

FAUSTUS

I am not a devil!

MEPH.

Well, you will be.

ENTER THE SULTAN AND HIS VIZIER, WHO CARRIES ON A
LARGE JAR AND SETS IT DOWN.

SULTAN

Good-morning, gentlemen. I trust you slept well.

FAUSTUS

Perfectly, sir. Your divans are exquisite.

SULTAN

I hope we may resume our frank discussion.

Tell me, why did you want to make gold?

FAUSTUS

For the challenge; for wealth; for trade; for beauty's
sake.

SULTAN

That covers everything, but tells me nothing.

FAUSTUS

Well then, perhaps it was the wrong question.

VIZIER

Too much wit in a guest is not appreciated.

SULTAN

Let him speak. He has a mind of his own.

FAUSTUS

I took all knowledge as my sea of dreams
And cast off into it. Making gold
Was by the way, a game, a joy of mind-play.
It was not quarry I was after, it was the chase.

The thrill of tracking a new element,
The thrill of tracking a new galaxy,
The thrill of finding hell in a new sunspot—

MEPH.

That was not hell. Hell is not material.

Hell is separation from something else—

FAUSTUS

Which you cannot name. All right. Correction:
The thrill of thinking sunspots were like hell –
The greater thrill of feeling myself grow
Like a huge tree from day to breaking day,
Branches, twigs, buds twitching and whispering
As they spread and sped into the unknown:
That was pure science, my lord Sultan.

VIZIER

Pure megalomania!

SULTAN

                                    Interesting though.
What do you think, Mephistopheles?

MEPH.

My friend Faustus is a learned man
Who is still learning. His mind does not stand still.
I have some knowledge I impart to him
Of places he has not yet visited
Though he will do so, as I believe.
I have friends of some standing; he meets them;
They give him thoughts he has not had before.

I am sure some signal destiny awaits him,

Though what and where it is remains to unfold.

VIZIER

My lord Sultan, we have heard much about science.

These big boys of the brain have miles to go

Before they reach even the foothills of wisdom.

Wisdom is of the east. We have it, know it,

Perhaps we can impart it. You, Mephistopheles,

Admit you cannot see into the future—

MEPH.

About twenty-four years, is that not so, my Faustus?

FAUSTUS

Aye, that is so.

VIZIER

— but we have a genie

Who can, and does. Once he's released from his jar

He is very dangerous. You must all be quiet.

He will unveil hundreds of years for you,

And tell you about the Seven Deadly Things.

THUNDER AND LIGHTNING, OR SOME SIMILAR COMMOTION.
SHRIEKS AND GROANS. SMOKE. THE GENIE'S VOICE IS HEARD
FROM THE JAR.

GENIE

Show yourselves, my dears. Make yourselves known.

FAUSTUS

Who are you, the first?

THALIDOMIDE

I am Thalidomide. My mother was a chemist in a white coat and my father was a banker in a dark suit. I love to dance and prance in the womb of a pregnant woman and pull her about, so that her baby emerges with no arms, or no legs, or one leg and one arm, or two shoulders with a fringe of tiny fingers like wings on them, just like an angel – O it is such fun!

FAUSTUS

A tall story, well told.

MEPH.

And you, the second, what are you?

ANTHRAX

I am Anthrax. My mother was an old spore and my father was a biological warrior. For many years I lived on an uninhabited island and quickly multiplied. I enjoyed having dead things round about me and am always looking for bodies to enter and destroy. Sheep and cattle used to be my favourites but I am into human beings now. It is great to watch the huge blebs and pustules spread and burn, and the life ebb away. I don't care if they are enemies or friends!

MEPH.

Nicely imagined, that.

FAUSTUS

The third one, what are you called?

LOBOTOMY

I am Lobotomy. My mother was a psychiatrist and my father was a brain surgeon. What I like is to see the brain being sliced up in different ways to discover how much you can do without. It's no use just trying to calm people down, you might as well pop them a tranquillizer. But to turn a person into a vegetable – that's terrific. Staring eyes and twitching lips, great stuff. That's what experiments are for.

FAUSTUS

That was entertaining.

MEPH.

Come now the fourth. Your name?

DEFOLIATION

I am Defoliation. I never knew my parents, but I'm told that once upon a time a spray-gun got familiar with a military map. At any rate, my specialty is getting poor peasants to actually starve to death. It's nice to see the leaves curling and dropping, that's quite artistic, but you have to wait to see the full effect. When all the crops fail and the bloated corpses bob along the river, that's the high point. Oh yes, animals and birds and insects die too, and it's a grand clear-out altogether.

MEPH.

Now there's a new thought.

FAUSTUS

And the fifth, who are you?

NAPALM

I am Napalm. My mother was called Jelly Belly and my father was called Pain Pain. I stick to you very close because I love you so much. You will never get rid of me. Even when your skin is flayed to strips, I embrace you, I am not put off

71

by pus or black crust. Let me set my lips on you and it will be the hottest kiss you ever had.

FAUSTUS

Crude but effective story.

MEPH.

Number six, declare yourself.

MELTDOWN

I am Meltdown. My father was a Dragon and my mother was the Queen of Uranium. I am very excitable and when I become over-heated I tear off my jacket and roar. It is wonderful to think how my foul breath radiates outwards invisibly for hundreds of miles and causes havoc among beasts and men. Best of all is to watch the leukaemia children wasting away on their iron beds.

MEPH.

Well presented.

FAUSTUS

Seventh and last, what are you?

NEUTRONBOMB

I am Neutronbomb. There was such a cluster of whitecoats round my cradle, chucking me under the chin, clucking and congratulating, that I never bothered to find out who my parents really were. But I was handled very carefully, and grew up with that love of the arts and hatred of people which is my consuming characteristic. My aim is a world of dead cities where nothing lives or moves, and the towers shine in the sun.

[GREAT COMMOTION AS ʋ

GENIE VANISHES. EVERYO

FUTURE, ADMIT IT', 'A LOA

AWFUL WARNING', ETC E1

FO

VIZIER

Now you have seen th

That trap for soaring ɪ

You Faustus, and you

Are keen to recommen

But you will not do it in this dominion.

You are yourselves forbidden from this moment.

You are a threat to Islam and the truth.

Under the powers I hold from my lord Sultan

I arrest you for corruption of the state.

FAUSTUS

[TO MEPH.] Invisibility – and go?

MEPH.

[TO FAUSTUS] Invisibility – and go?

THEY THROW ON THEIR CLOAKS OF INVISIBILITY AND

DISAPPEAR. VIZIER AND SULTAN ARE STARTLED BUT RECOVER

QUICKLY.

SULTAN

It is well seen that they were only spirits,

Sent here to tempt us by the Evil One.

I must say I have a soft spot for the doctor.

It is his companion leads him astray.

VIZIER

They are two h

Destruction

As it has

SULTAN

alves of the same terrible coin.

strides among us, bearing gifts

done since time began.

Well, well.

EXEUNT

## Act Five *Scene One*

ENTER WAGNER, READING A DOCUMENT

WAGNER

I think my master means to die shortly,
For in his will he leaves me all his goods.
Strange though, he still makes merry with the students,
Drinking and talking the small hours away.
Since he came back from Constantinople
He seems so restless, almost feverish.
I worry about him. – But here he comes.

EXIT

ENTER FAUSTUS, MEPHISTOPHELES, AND A SCHOLAR

SCHOLAR

Good doctor, we students had a long discussion on 'Who
was the most beautiful woman in the world?' and we came to
the conclusion that it was Helen of Troy. Would you not use
that great art of illusion which you and your companion have
perfected, and show us Helen as she was?

FAUSTUS

> I will. It is a fair request. I know you wish me well, and like a
> good friend I shall do what I can for you. You will see her as
> Sir Paris saw her when he brought those unmatched spoils of
> war to Troy.

SCHOLAR

> I think she was well worth that ten years war the Greeks
> spent trying to avenge her abduction. An amazing
> woman. Thank you Dr Faustus. We shall speak again
> soon.

FAUSTUS

> You are welcome.

EXIT SCHOLAR

ENTER AN OLD MAN

OLD MAN

> O gentle Faustus, let Helen rest in peace!
> The arts you practise lead you to damnation.
> You are tempted always to go further, further,
> But only devils are so single-minded.
> You have a generous and kindly soul;
> Don't let repeated badness change its nature.
> For if it does, repentance comes too late,
> And you will never see the face of heaven.
> The pains of hell are not to be spoken of.
> Dear son, you must not think my earnestness

Is meant to cut or harm you; what I say
Is spoken not in anger but from love,
From tender love, from pity of what might come
If you court only endless misery.
Believe me, I wish you only endless good.

FAUSTUS

What have I done? How near is the abyss?
I think I must be damned, and ought to die.

MEPH. GIVES HIM A DAGGER

I hear a roaring voice that tells me hell
Has come to claim its right. 'Faustus,' it says,
'Your hour-glass has run out, come quickly' –
And if I die the bargain is complete.

[FAUSTUS GOES TO USE THE DAGGER]

OLD MAN

Stop, good Faustus, you are too desperate!
I see an angel hovering overhead
Ready to pour a precious vial of grace
Down upon your thirsty beleaguered soul.
Call out for mercy, and avoid despair.

FAUSTUS

My friend, there is some comfort in your words.
Leave me awhile, to ponder on my sins.

OLD MAN

All right, but it is with a heavy heart
I leave you to the enemy of the soul.

EXIT

FAUSTUS

Where is there mercy? I live under a curse.
I do repent, and yet I do despair.
Hell and grace like snakes fight in my breast.
What can I do to shun the snares of death?

MEPH.

Faustus, you are a traitor. Didn't you swear
Allegiance to my great lord Lucifer?
Do you want me to tear your flesh to pieces?

FAUSTUS

I do repent if I offended him.
Sweet Mephistopheles, entreat your lord
To pardon all my unjust backslidings.
I'll use my blood again and reconfirm
The former vow I made to Lucifer.

MEPH.

Do it then quickly, and make sure you mean it,
Unless you want to drift into worse dangers.

FAUSTUS

That old man: The wretch persuaded me
To turn from Lucifer. Torture him,
Sweet friend, with every cruelty in hell.

MEPH.

His faith is great, I cannot touch his soul.
But what I can afflict his body with
I'll try. It isn't worth much, but I'll try.

FAUSTUS

Good servant, there is still one thing I crave,
To glut the longing of my heart's desire:
Give me, to be with me as my lover,
That heavenly Helen who passed by us here,
And her embraces will soon snuff and smother
Any thoughts I have that might dissuade me
From being true to Lucifer and my oath.

MEPH.

This, or what else my Faustus may request,
Shall happen in the twinkling of an eye.

ENTER HELEN AGAIN

FAUSTUS

Was this the face that launched a thousand ships
And burnt the heaven-hidden towers of Troy?
Sweet Helen, make me immortal with a kiss!
Her lips suck out my soul, see where it flies!
Come, Helen, come, give me my soul again.
My home is here, divinity in these lips.
All that's not Helen is but a dead world.
I will be Paris, and for love of you
I will sack Wittenberg instead of Troy;
Take arms against that feeble Menelaus,
And plant your colours in my helmet-plume;
I'll wound Achilles in his Achilles heel,
And then return to Helen for a kiss.
Oh you are fairer than the evening air

Clad in the beauty of a thousand stars:
Brighter than the naked lightnings of Jupiter
Consuming hapless lovers; and more lovely
Than that shimmering dazzle of the sun-god
Lured into a fountain by its spirit.
And you, and only you, shall be my lover.

EXEUNT FAUSTUS AND HELEN


Act Five *Scene Two*

ENTER FAUSTUS AND WAGNER

FAUSTUS

Well, Wagner, you have read my will right through?
How does it seem to you?

WAGNER

It is a marvel
Of thoughtfulness. Sir, while I live
You have my love, devotion, service.

FAUSTUS

Thanks Wagner.

EXIT WAGNER

ENTER THREE SCHOLARS

Welcome gentlemen.

I SCHOLAR

Good Faustus, you look different, you look changed.

FAUSTUS

Ah gentlemen!

**2 SCHOLAR**

What is wrong, dear Faustus?

**FAUSTUS**

Ah my friend, my close friend of old, if I still shared rooms with you I would be a living man still, but now I am as if dead, and dead for ever. Look sirs, is that not him – there – coming for me?

**1 SCHOLAR**

O my dear Faustus, what are you afraid of?

**2 SCHOLAR**

Has all your pleasure given way to sadness?

**3 SCHOLAR**

He has made himself ill by being too solitary.

**2 SCHOLAR**

If that's the case we shall find doctors for him.

**3 SCHOLAR**

You've been overdoing things, sir, that's all.

**FAUSTUS**

Overdoing deadly sin, damning both body and soul.

**2 SCHOLAR**

God's mercy is infinite, Faustus, look to that.

**FAUSTUS**

But mine is the offence that cannot be pardoned. The serpent that tempted Eve may be saved, but not Faustus. Ah gentlemen, be patient, listen to me, and do not shiver at what I say, though my heart pants and shivers to remember that I have studied here for thirty years – If only I had never seen

Wittenberg, never read a book – and what wonders I have done, all Germany knows, all the world indeed – and for this I have lost both Germany and the world – yes, heaven itself – heaven, the seat of God, the kingdom of joy – and must remain in hell for over – hell, ah hell, for ever! Sweet friends, what shall become of Faustus, being in hell for ever?

2 SCHOLAR

Call on God, Faustus, call on God still!

FAUSTUS

On God, whom I abjured? On God, whom I blasphemed? Ah my God! – I would weep, if the devil had not drawn in my tears. It should be blood – life and soul – instead of tears – but oh, he stops my tongue! If I try to lift my arms up, see, look, they hold them, they hold them!

ALL

Who, Faustus?

FAUSTUS

Don't you know? – Lucifer and Mephistopheles. Ah gentlemen, I gave them my soul for my science.

ALL

God forbid!

FAUSTUS

God forbade it indeed, but Faustus did it. For the empty pleasures of twenty-four years I gave up eternal joy and happiness. I wrote them a document with my own blood; the date is expired, this is the time; and he will fetch me.

**1 SCHOLAR**

Why did you not tell us this before, when ministers might have prayed for you?

**FAUSTUS**

I often thought of doing so, but the devil threatened to tear me to pieces if I mentioned God, to fetch me body and soul if I once spoke well of divinity; and now it is too late. Leave me, gentlemen, in case you perish with me.

**2 SCHOLAR**

O what can we do to save you?

**FAUSTUS**

Forget me; save yourselves; leave me.

**3 SCHOLAR**

I'll stay with Faustus; God will strengthen me.

**1 SCHOLAR**

Sweet friend, you must not tempt God. Come with us all into the next room, where at least we can pray for him.

**FAUSTUS**

Aye, pray for me; and no matter what noise you may hear, do not come through to me, for nothing can rescue me.

**2 SCHOLAR**

It is our prayer, and it must be yours, that God may have mercy.

**FAUSTUS**

Goodnight then, gentlemen, and goodbye. If I live till morning, I'll visit you: if not, I'll be in hell.

ALL

Goodnight and goodbye, Faustus.

EXEUNT SCHOLARS

THE CLOCK STRIKES ELEVEN

FAUSTUS

Ah Faustus,
Now you have only one bare hour to live,
And then you must be damned perpetually.
Stand still, you stars, you fires, you mechanisms,
Get time to stop, and midnight never come.
May the sun rise, and rise again, and make
Perpetual day; or stretch this hour into
A year, a month, a week, a natural day,
Time to repent, a day to save my soul.
Drive slowly, slowly, horses of the night!
The stars move still, time runs, the clock will strike,
The devil will come, and then I must be damned.
O I'll leap up to my God! Who pulls me down?
See, see where Christ's blood streams across the sky! –
One drop would save my soul, a half-drop, ah my Christ –
Let me name him, call on him, spare me Lucifer!
Where is it now? Gone; and only God
Stretches out his arm and frowns and points.
Mountains and hills, come here and fall on me,
Hide me from the terrible anger of God.
No no, they won't, I know they will not come.
Earth then, break open! No, it rejects me.

You stars I was born under, figured only
To have me conveyed towards death and hell,
Draw me up now like a thick sprawl of mist
Into the labouring belly of a cloud
And then expel me from it in a storm,
So that although my shattered limbs are lost
My soul may still be free to fly to heaven.

### CLOCK STRIKES THE HALF-HOUR

Ah, half the hour is past, the rest comes soon!
O God,
If you will not have mercy on my soul,
Yet for the sake of Christ, ransomer of souls,
Impose some end to my incessant pain:
Suppose I live in hell a thousand years,
A hundred thousand, let me be saved at last!
No, there's no limit: it goes on for ever.
Far better to be born without a soul,
Or to believe in reincarnation and have your soul
Migrate at death into a beast: the beast
Is happy, dies earthbound, earth-nourishing.
Only man is to be plagued in hell.
I curse my parents that they ever had me!
No no, it's me I curse, or Lucifer
Who has deprived me of the joys of heaven.

### CLOCK STRIKES TWELVE

It strikes, it strikes! O body, turn to air,
Or hellish arms will wrap themselves around you.

O soul, dissolve yourself in drops of water
And fall into the all-concealing sea.

My God, my God! O stare less fiercely on me!
Monstrous shapes, let me breathe, one breath!
Let it not be hell, let it not be Lucifer!
I'll burn my books – ah Mephistopheles!

EXEUNT WITH HIM


Act Five *Scene Three*

ENTER THE SCHOLARS

1 SCHOLAR

Well gentlemen, the night is over, and Faustus is dead.

2 SCHOLAR

I wish we could say he was at peace.

3 SCHOLAR

Do you not think we might have saved him?

2 SCHOLAR

He expressly told us not to interfere, whatever we heard.

1 SCHOLAR

It was a dreadful night, but there was more than wind
and storm at work. Those flashing lights, and the shrieks
and cries! At one time the whole building seemed to be
on fire.

3 SCHOLAR

Well, if it was the devils he spoke of, they have triumphed.

We do not know. We have the poor shell of his mortal remains, and it is our duty to give this a decent burial. All our students shall wear black on that occasion. He was a scholar of great note, and Germany was rightly proud of him. May his love of knowledge and science not be lost with his departure.

EXEUNT

# Epilogue

ENTER CHORUS IV

CHORUS

    Cut is the branch that might have grown so straight.
    Burned is the laurel bough of genius
    That flourished once within this learned man.
    His story like a lightning-flash invades
    The dark heart of complacency, and we
    Who watch the darkness settle down once more
    Remember, and will remember, those green thoughts
    That wait to break through stone where Faustus sleeps.

EXIT